E. J. Cowley

The Bohemians

E. J. Cowley

The Bohemians

ISBN/EAN: 9783337863333

Printed in Europe, USA, Canada, Australia, Japan

Cover: Foto ©Thomas Meinert / pixelio.de

More available books at **www.hansebooks.com**

THE BOHEMIANS

A COMEDY IN THREE ACTS

BY

E. J. COWLEY

BOSTON

1896

THE BOHEMIANS.

CHARACTERS.

JACK BRANDT......................................*An Artist.*
NOEL BLAKE......................................*A Composer.*
JIM DALE..*A Sculptor.*
GEO. SMILEY.....................................*A Musician.*
MAJOR WRANGLE...................................*An Adventurer.*
FREDDIE SPROUL..................................*An Art Student.*
BERTIE FOLLET...................................*An Exquisite.*
SAM...*A Servant.*
MADGE HARDY.....................................*An Orphan.*
MRS. VAN SLICK..............................*A Lady of Fashion.*
BLANCHE VAN SLICK...............................*Her Daughter.*
MRS. KENNET.....................................*A Governess.*
VAN...*A St. Bernard Dog.*

Costumes Modern.

COSTUMES.

JACK.—Velvet coat and vest, dark pants. Same throughout the play, but very poor and seedy in the last act.

NOEL.—*1st Act.*—Same as Jack. *2d Act.*—Stylish summer suit. *3d Act.*—Dark suit, tall hat, etc.

MAJOR WRANGLE.—Stylish suit, changing with the acts.

DALE AND SMILEY.—*1st Act.*—Stylish suits. *2d Act.*—Outing suits. *3d Act.*—Stylish suits.

FREDDIE SPROUL.—*1st Act.*—Velvet coat and vest. *2d and 3d Acts.* —Dark suit.

BERTIE FOLLET.—Foppish dress.

SAM.—Dark suit, white vest.

MADGE.—*1st Act.*—Gray dress. *2d Act.*—Stylish summer gown. *3d Act.*—Stylish winter gown, which she changes to first dress.

MRS. VAN SLICK and MISS BLANCHE.—Stylish throughout play.

MRS. KENNET.—Simple costume.

PROPERTIES.

ACT 1ST.—Table, chairs, piano, bouquet, easel, sketches, pictures, newspaper, basket of strawberries, rolls of music, money.

ACT 2D.—Gun to be loaded, picnic lay-out, sketch-book and pencil.

ACT 3D.—Same as act first, with the addition of champagne for SPROUL and the dog.

PRINTING.

The following stand and window printing, advertising this play, may be had of the houses named below. *We do not carry this printing in stock nor furnish it.*

GREAT WESTERN SHOW PRINT.
511 MARKET ST., ST. LOUIS, MO.
THREE SHEETS.

No. 154, suitable for Bertie Follet.
" 290, " " Noel Blake.
" 153, " " Smiley.
" 291, " " Beresford.
" 481, " " Jack.

HALF SHEET WINDOW LITHOGRAPHS.
Nos. 1168, 1014, 1024, 404, 850, 468, and 496.

EMPIRE SHOW PRINT.
75 PLYMOUTH PLACE, CHICAGO.
THREE SHEETS.

No. 82, suitable for Second Act.
" 94, " " Madge.
" 101, " " Blanche.
" 107, " " Noel and Madge.
" 134, " " Madge.

CENTRAL SHOW PRINT, CHICAGO.
No. 184, suitable for Dale.
" 183, " " Mrs. Van Slick.

THE BOHEMIANS.

ACT I.

Scene.—JACK BRANDT'S *studio. A plain room. Window* R. C. *in flat; door* L. C., *also* R. *and* L. *2d and 3d entrance. Piano up stage* L. *Table at window in flat. Easel with unfinished picture* R. I E. *Pictures and sketches around room; work basket on table. Music for curtain. Stage discovered empty at rise. Knock outside twice. Then* FREDDY SPROUL *puts his head in* L. C. *and looks around; enters cautiously; has a large bouquet of flowers in his hand.*

Fred. (*looking around*). She is not here! Good! For I can now leave my bouquet without any fear of being found out. (*Puts bouquet on table.*) I wonder if she ever suspects where they come from? Sometimes I almost hope she does. But no, I am sure she has not the slightest idea. For when she meets me, she holds out her hand so carelessly and says, "Good-morning, Mr. Sproul," so calmly, that she throws me down into the lowest depths of despair again. Twice this week have I screwed my courage up to the sticking point in order to tell her how much I love her, but when she turned her great limpid eyes upon me, blow me if I couldn't feel all of my courage ooze out at the tips of my fingers again. (*Starts.*) I've got an idea. (*Looks around and takes picture out of his pocket.*) Here is a small portrait of myself that I have just painted, and I will just place it here in the bouquet (*business of putting picture in bouquet*) and let it speak for me. There, I have done it at last (MADGE *sings outside*), and here she is coming now. (*Comes down.*) Lord! how my heart does beat.

    [*Entrance music for* MADGE, *who enters quickly* L.C., *with a basket of strawberries on her arm. Places basket on table; speaks while taking off hat and wraps.*

Madge. Ah! Good-morning, Mr. Sproul.

5

Fred. (*confused and stammers in speech*). Goo—goo—good-morning, M—M—Miss Hardy. (*Aside.*) Just the same as usual.   [*Goes down* R. 1 E.

Madge (*goes to table ; prepares to pick over her straw-berries ; speaks during preparations*). Waiting to see Jack, I suppose. I am very sorry that he is not in. (*Draws chair, seats herself with her side to audience, and begins work on berries.*) He has gone to inquire about poor Mr. Warner, who, you know, is lying very ill at his home ; but I expect him back now 'most any moment. You don't mind my going on with my work, do you, Mr. Sproul ? You see, Noel has not got up yet, but he will be wanting his breakfast when he does rise, so I wish to have those strawberries ready for him. You don't mind, do you ?   [*Laughingly.*

Fred. (*in a confused manner*). Why, no—of course, Miss Madge. That is—I mean—oh, yes, go right on. Don't mind me. (*Aside.*) I wish I had that picture back again.

Madge. Are you having a holiday, Mr. Sproul ?

Fred. Oh, no. Why did you ask that ?

Madge. Oh, for nothing in particular. I only imagined you must be taking a holiday, else you would not be around so early.

Fred. No ! Well—that is—you see, Miss Madge, the matter was I could not sleep ; I had a bad toothache all night long, so I thought I'd take a walk, and as I was passing I just looked in.

Madge (*reproachfully*). Oh ! But you are losing the best hours of the morning, and that is such a pity. I thought you were determined to become a great artist, like Jack ; and how can you do that unless you work hard ? Jack, you know, is never idle.

Fred. That is quite true, Miss Madge ; and yet he does not seem to make much progress with his great picture up there. [*Points to picture on wall* L., *and crosses over and exam-ines it at conclusion of speech.*

Madge (*turning and looking at it*). Ah, true, the poor fel-low.   [*Spoken sadly.*

Fred. (*examining picture*). "Cleopatra Awaiting the Com-ing of Octavius," I believe he calls it, and (*laughing*) by the looks of things she seems to have been waiting a long, long time. Why, the picture is actually smothered with dust.

Madge (*spirited*). And all because I am not tall enough to reach it, and Jack will not allow me to stand upon a chair for fear I might fall and hurt myself. (*Spoken more sadly.*) And when I speak to him about finishing it, he only laughs and says it can afford to wait. You see it takes all of his time painting those little sketches—pot-boilers, he calls them—in order to get money enough to run the house ; and so, you see, in the meantime his great picture, of which he used to dream so fondly, remains there, forgotten and unfinished.

[*Bows her head on table.*

Fred. (*crossing quickly*). There, there, Miss Madge, please don't feel so badly about it. I didn't mean anything like that when I spoke. I don't wish to cast a slur upon dear old Jack. Now, don't cry any more ; and please say that you will forgive me, for, 'pon my honor, I didn't mean anything.

Madge (*drying her eyes*). I am sure you didn't. (*Rises.*) And there is my hand. (*Offers hand, which* FRED. *takes.*) I feel a little bit nervous this morning. But don't mind me ; and now that I have my strawberries all picked, Noel can get up as soon as he pleases. (*Is crossing to* L.; *noise outside ; she turns and runs to door* L. C.) And here comes Jack now, I believe. [*Opens door,* L. C.

Enter SMILEY *and* DALE.

Smiley. Good-morning, Miss Madge. Can we come in ?

Madge. Why, certainly. Come right along.

[*They both point at* FRED., *who is down* R.; *then both go down, one on each side of him, slap him on the back and grasp his hands. Business ad libitum.*

Smiley *and* **Dale** (*together*). What, old chappie ! Delighted to meet you.

Madge. Oh, boys, please don't make such a noise. Noel is asleep.

Smiley *and* **Dale** (*run up towards back,* L., *with* FRED. *between them*). Then we will wake him up.

Madge (*stopping them*). Oh, no ; you mustn't do that, for you know it always makes him cross and irritable to rouse him from his sleep in that manner, and then you know how very sensitive he is.

Dale. Oh, yes, we know, and for your sake, Miss Madge, we will not disturb his dreams, more especially when a fellow has such dreams as he does.

Smiley (*who has been examining picture on wall* L.). I say, Dale, old man, come here and look at this. By Jove, how it progresses. How hard the old boy does work.

Madge. That makes the second time this morning that Jack's picture has been held up to ridicule for his lack of industry. But, you see, Jack's work is for the present, not for the future.

Dale. There, Miss Madge, you are down upon us like a ton of brick. We really did not mean to underrate Jack's good intentions. Now, I confess that I am a lazy, idle fellow myself ; but, really, what is the use of one killing one's self in these degenerate days of taste in art ? Now, why did I leave my sculptor's studio ? Was it for lack of patronage ? Oh, no ; but because the people who came to see me insisted upon my accomplishing the most absurd things. I must straighten this one's nose, I must give that one an eye for the one it had lost, and I must put the face of a Greek god in the place of the one brought me to work from, which, perhaps, was so ugly that it gave you a pain in the face to look at it. Now, for instance, suppose that Fred. Sproul there should order a bust of himself. What on earth could I do with such material?

[*Crosses* R. *to* FRED.; *business.*

Smiley. And as for me, Miss Madge, when I offered my compositions to a brainless public, they failed to understand either my music or my lines or the message which they intended to convey. Thus things went on until I was actually reduced to a state bordering upon beggary ; until one day Dale came into my rooms, where I was hard at work upon a new composition, and throwing down a bundle of doggerel rhymes upon the table, said to me, "Smiley, old man, I have a bright idea. I have thrown down the sculptor's mallet and chisel forever. You have always praised my singing powers and have urged me to go on the stage. I have at last made up my mind to follow your advice. Compose for me some light, catchy music to those verses that I have written myself, and I will make you immortal."

Dale. And most nobly have I kept my word, for to-day our songs are sung by stage artists all over the world, and in every music store you will find our compositions, whilst in the homes of the rich and poor alike our names are household words. And that brings us to the object of our visit here this morning. We have just completed a new three-act comic opera, and knowing your talent as a singer and also your eagerness to find something to do that will help lighten Jack's load of care, we wish to make some arrangements with you, if possible, to play the leading rôle in the first presentation of the piece next month.

Madge. Oh, I am so grateful to you both for your kindness. But you know that while, thanks to Noel, I am in your estimation good enough to trust the leading singing rôle to, I know nothing about acting.

Smiley. So much the better. The less you know about a thing nowadays the better you are appreciated.

Dale. Oh, no, Miss Madge, you possess a charm more potent with the public, and to which it pays a much higher tribute nowadays than it does to the art of acting.

Madge. And what is that, pray ?

Smiley. First, a pleasing and well-cultivated voice.

Dale. A very pretty face.

Smiley. Third and last, but by no means least—in fact, it is the most potent of all the other charms you possess put together —you have an elegant figure.

Dale. And you know the music as well as we do, for it is simply a different arrangement of our oldest songs. And now, while Jack is away, just let us run through a few of the numbers. We can press Fred into service also for this occasion.
[*Business ad libitum then introduced.*

Smiley (*after specialties are ended*). Bravo! It couldn't be better, Madge; you are a regular daisy. (*Goes to table, picks up and smells bouquet; discovers picture.*) Ah, what a lovely bouquet. What is this—some new admirer, Miss Madge? [*All look at it.*

Fred. (*down R., nervously; aside*). Oh, Lord! I am done for now, sure.

Madge. Oh, no; I never saw it before. What can it be?

Dale (*who has come down to* FRED.). Rash youth, what have you done! If Jack should discover your penchant——

Jack (*outside*). Come here, you rascal!

Dale (*all turn*). And here he comes now.

Jack (*outside; speaks to dog while* MADGE *has door partly open. At conclusion of the speech,* MADGE *throws door open and* JACK **enters**). Lie down there, you rascal, and don't leave that spot. Remember you have an appointment with me at two o'clock. I want you to sit for me.

Enters; MADGE *clings to him and helps him to remove his coat while he speaks.*

Jack. Hello, Smiley! (*Shakes hands.*) And Dale, old boy, how goes it with you? (*Same business; going to* MADGE.) And how is my little busy bee? Still working, I suppose?

Madge. Not very hard, Jack. But tell me, how did you find poor Warner?

Jack. Much better; and the babies have all had a good breakfast from the basket you sent them, dear. So now I can get to my work with an easy mind. (*Arranges easel.*) Well, Smiley, where are you and Dale off to this fine morning?
[*Takes off coat and puts on blouse.*

Dale. Oh, we thought we would take a short trip on the river, and called to get Noel to go with us, when, lo and behold, we find that he is asleep.

Jack (*at easel*). Well, then, let him sleep. He says his best ideas come to him while he sleeps. Now, why not take Sproul with you instead? (*Going up to table.*) He never seems to me to have anything in particular to do. (*Picks up picture.*) Hello, Madge, what have we here?

Smiley. That is just what we were trying to find out when you came in. Whose head is it?

Jack (*looking hard at* FREDDY SPROUL). Are you sure it is a head ? I think it must be intended for a landscape.

[*All laugh ;* FRED. *is annoyed.*

Dale. Well, Smiley, after that we might as well be off. Come, Sproul.

Fred. Really, now——

Smiley (*grasps him*). No excuses ; you have got to come. Good-morning, Miss Madge. Same to you, old man.

Dale. And if we have but succeeded in making our amateur artist here thoroughly unhappy, we feel that we have not wholly wasted an idle hour.   [**Exeunt** C., *with* FRED.

Enter NOEL *from room* L. 3 E., *yawning.*

Madge (*confused*). Oh, Noel, I hope those noisy fellows did not disturb you. But I forgot for the time that you were asleep.

Noel. That pair are such fools, kicking up such a row at this hour.   [*Sits at piano.*

Jack (*at easel*). Hello, Noel, up already ?

Noel. Well, and why shouldn't I be up as well as you ?

Jack. Why not, to be sure ? But then, you see, you are not obliged to profit by the daylight for your work, as I am, or to get breakfast like our little busy bee there. He is in one of his dejected moods this morning ; give him a scolding, Madge.

Madge (*rising*). I smell the coffee boiling, so I will give him his breakfast first, so as not to take an unfair advantage of him. (*Gives him paper.*) Here is the paper, and I will have your breakfast ready in a few moments.   [**Exit** R. 3 E.

Jack (*looking after her*). Bless her bright face ! It is not for nothing that she lives so near the sun in this dingy attic up here.

Noel. Say, Jack, did you ever hear of an eccentric individual named Gale ?

Jack. Never. Why ?

Noel. He is dead ; that is all. Here is what is in this morning's paper. (*Reads.*) " The musical world has sustained a serious loss in the sudden death of Mr. Wm. Gale, one of the most ardent and eccentric amateurs in this country."

Jack. A musical amateur, eh ? One chance the less for you, old boy, more's the pity.

Noel. But what a windfall for his heirs ! (*Reads.*) " The fortune of the deceased is estimated at one-half a million of dollars. He was unmarried, and leaves no one but distant relatives to mourn his loss." (*Throws down paper and comes down* L.) By Jove ! what luck some people do have.

Jack. True, my boy ; you and I, for instance.

Noel. You and I ! Surely you do not consider yourself lucky.

Jack. Don't I? Indeed, then, but I do; and why not? Now, in the first place, I have the honor of being an honest man. I neither bother my head about politics or the money market; I don't go into society; and the crowning point of all is, I am the intimate friend of the great composer, Noel Blake; and now what more could I wish for?

Noel. Money! *[Sits on stool at piano.*

Jack. Money! Why, haven't we got money? There is five dollars still in the bank, to say nothing of a quarter or so still in my vest pocket. Money, indeed! You young Sardanapalus!

Noel (*rises*). Oh, it's all very well, Jack, for you to make light of our poverty; but you cannot imagine my feelings when I think that I am living off your scanty earnings; that I am actually forced to accept your bounty. *[Bows head on piano.*

Jack. Yes; there you go again! What a great creature I am to be sure; a regular paragon of friendship. That is all understood, so don't say any more about it.

Noel. I tell you I can't help it. Don't I see you wasting your life and your talents day by day in the useless task you have undertaken? Do you think I am deceived by your careless tone? Haven't I heard you sigh time and again when your eyes have turned wearily from those pot-boilers and fallen upon the sketch of your great picture over there? The one dream of your life, for the fulfilment of which you can never find time. And what, if after all this great and useless sacrifice on your part, the greater artist of us two should turn out to be yourself.

Jack (*rises from easel, comes* C., *and while talking, draws out and lights pipe*). The old story, my lad. Now, the whole thing in a nutshell is simply this: There were two empty purses between us, and we joined them together and made one out of them. You couldn't make a decent living for yourself and your cousin Madge by your music pupils, and yet they absorbed all of the time that might be given to some great composition. I was compelled every now and then to leave the picture over there upon which I was working for one of those little commercial transactions you are pleased to call pot-boilers, and neither of us seemed to advance one step.

Noel. Yes, I know all that, but——

Jack. Well, I looked the matter square in the face, and I said to myself: Noel and I have a wall to climb; the ladder is long and the wind is high; if we both mount together, the ladder will break. Let Noel go up first, whilst I hold the ladder steady against the wall, and when he has reached the top in safety, he can lend me a helping hand in return.

Noel. Well, thanks to your holding the ladder, as you call it, I have found time to write a symphony which you pronounce great, and have offered it to the Philharmonic Society for production ; and though it has been in their hands now for over three months, they have not condescended to give it a hearing yet.

Jack. Patience, lad, patience. The symphony is written anyhow, and has my approval. Madge is also charmed with it ; and do you remember how very delighted that old man was—the noble stranger, as we called him—when he heard you play it that evening ?

Noel. Some old lunatic. By Jove ! the way he entered the room was decidedly suggestive of a strait-jacket.

Jack (*crosses to easel*). Ay, but the exit that he made more than redeemed his character. " Here is fifty dollars on account, Mr. Brandt," he said, when he ordered the picture there (*points to easel*), and the speech struck me as being a damned eloquent one. But, by the way, Noel, lad, take that sketch over there to Old Screwsby ; it will bring a couple of dollars, I think, and I promised Warner's wife this morning I would send her around some wine for him this afternoon.

Noel. My God ! another starving genius ! Oh, it is infamous ! While a set of numbskulls and idiots are rolling in wealth, here are three men of genius—Warner, you, and myself—actually denied a living. One dying from hunger, another cannot find time to develop the gift Heaven gave him, whilst the third is even denied a hearing from the public ! Oh, the thought drives me wild !

Jack. Noel, my lad, I am afraid that you have a grain of envy in your composition. Beware of that, my boy, for it is an evil weed and will grow up apace, and will sap and choke up the good growth in your heart unless you pluck it out. Now, only suppose a fortune was suddenly thrust upon you, what would you do with it ? How many times a day would you dine, and how many suits of clothes would you wear ?

Noel. Well, Jack, if I were rich, I would be content to dine once a day, and to wear but one pair of boots (*coming over* R.), but I could give you an order for a picture that would cost five thousand dollars.

Jack. Ah !

Noel. Yes, and I would send the same amount to poor Warner.

Jack. Good !

Noel. I would have my symphony produced in a theatre of my own.

Jack. Bravo !

Noel. And now, dear old boy, I am going to open my heart to you and show you the real cause of this fever of unrest—I could then marry the girl I love.

Jack (*looks up from easel and whistles*). What ! you in love ! (*Laughs.*) Well, upon my word, but that is the last straw.

Madge (*outside*). Are you tired of waiting, Noel ?

Noel. Hush !

Madge (*entering with breakfast*). Well, Noel, here is your breakfast at last. (*Prepares table.*) The toast browned to a turn, and I want you to just try those delicious strawberries. (*Coming down to* JACK.) Just try them, Jack. (*He refuses.*) Why, what is the matter ?

Jack (*rising*). I have lost my appetite for berries, little one. (*Goes to door* C. *and whistles.*) Come here, you rascal. (*Whistles.*) Blame me, but the rascal has run away.

[*Comes down.*

Madge. Shall I go after him, Jack ?

Jack. Yes, if you will, sunlight. (MADGE *runs for her things.*) I can't get the rascal to sit for me, but perhaps you will have more influence with him.

Madge (*tying on hat*). Well, I will try. You see, I will appeal to his good sense, and tell him how he is delaying your work. I can always reason with Van.　　　　　[**Exit** L. C.

Jack (*comes up ; looks off after her*). And now, Noel, that my little ruse has got Madge out of the way, let us have it. (*Sits on back of chair ; fills and lights pipe.*) You were going to tell me about your love affair. Who is it you are in love with ?

Noel. With Madge.

Jack (*surprised ; drops and breaks pipe*). What ! with Madge, your own cousin—our child ?

Noel. You know, Jack, although she calls me cousin, that there is no relationship between us ; and, although she was but a mere child when her guardian, my father, died and left her to my care, you seem to forget that in the five years that have passed since Madge has been transformed from a child of twelve years into a beautiful young woman.

Jack (*crossing to easel*). True ; but do you think she suspects ? Has she any idea of this feeling upon your part—that you love her ?

Noel. Well, I don't know. I have never said a word about it to her ; for what would be the good of it ? I am too poor to think of marrying any one.

Jack. You are right ; you are too poor to think of marriage. But, say, are you not going out to get that money for me ? I want to get some wine with it and send it to Warner.

Noel (*sits on piano stool and bows head on piano. Speaks the following in that position*). No, I don't think I will go out this morning. In fact, I don't feel like doing anything to-day.

Jack (*comes up and speaks harshly*). Not to-day alone, but, by Jove, every day. You would rather see me leave my work, so that you could sit around doing nothing. I told Mrs. Warner she should have the wine, and she is expecting it.

Noel (*jumps up, gets hat and pictures quickly ; shows that he is angry*). Say no more about it, I'll go. But, hang it, you needn't take on that tone of voice. I am only too well aware that you look upon me as an idle, useless fellow, who has been the chief cause of all your trouble.   [**Exit** L. C.

Jack (*coming down*). Noel gone with tears in his eyes and a sob in his voice ! What the devil has got into me anyway ? What made me speak to the boy in the manner that I did ? Can it really be that I, Jack Brandt, am jealous ? (*Laughs.*) Oh, nonsense ! that would be a good joke. Jack Brandt in love ! Oh, no ; love is not for the likes of me. I was born to play uncle to some other fellow's nurslings. (*Sighs and crosses to easel.*) Only let me see Noel happy and famous and I will be content to find my happiness in applauding his works and dancing his children on my knee ; and, by Jove, it was time for this confidence of Noel's, for it has at last opened my eyes. I don't know where I have not been wandering in my stupid, selfish dreams.

Enter MADGE.

Madge. Oh, Jack, it is really too bad, but I could not get Van to come home with me either by coaxing or talking sense to him.   [*Takes off her wraps.*

Jack. Never mind, little one ; perhaps it is all for the best, as I wish to talk to you all alone.

Madge. Oh, Jack, what about ?

Jack. Well, I want to know whether you love your cousin Noel or not.

Madge (*laughs*). What a funny question. (*Crosses to him ; leans on his back.*) Why, of course I do. I would be the most ungrateful girl in the world if I did not. When my father died, you remember, he left me to the care of his dearest friend, Noel's father, and no father could be kinder while he lived. After his death, I was left a homeless, fatherless child to Noel's care, and he has been very kind to me ever since. I was nothing to you, yet you have been as kind and considerate as Noel, and I love you, too, you dear old Jack.

Jack. Oh, yes, I was kind ; but you see, you don't know me ; I had a reason for my show of kindness.

Madge (*coming around and kneeling*, R.). Ah, Jack, do you imagine I don't understand, now that I have grown to be a woman ? Do you imagine I do not remember how you would come to visit Noel and myself in our miserable little garret on one pretext or another, but always bringing some small token in the shape of money or eatables to help us along, until at last you proposed that we should come and share your home with you ? This is what you have done for me (*rising*), and then you ask me if I love Noel.

Jack. Well, I confess, the question was a stupid one. But what I wished to call your attention to was, have you noticed anything strange about him ? Have you noticed lately how unhappy and depressed he appears ?

Madge. Oh, yes, but I did not wish to speak of it. Oh, Jack, is there anything the matter—has he any secret trouble ?

Jack. Well, I should say he had a secret trouble. Why, Madge, he is in love.

Madge (*surprised*). In love !—Noel in love ! Did he tell you so ?

Jack. Yes, not ten minutes ago.

Madge. Then why is he so unhappy ? Is it because she does not love him in return ?

Jack. Oh, no, indeed. In fact, the poor child is over head and ears in love with him herself, though she does not know it. She is such an innocent little darling that she mistakes her love for affection and friendship ; yet she is jealous of him and turns pale at the very thought of his marrying another. (*Dog barks and man shouts outside.*) Hello ! Some one has found Van at home.

> [*Racket is repeated ; then* MAJOR *enters quickly and shuts the door after him, holding it as if to keep some one out.*

Major. Excuse me for entering so unceremoniously, but there being no knocker on your door, and finding the key in the lock upon the outside, I took it for granted that your visitors were in the habit of entering unannounced. (*Aside.*) By Jove ! what a pretty girl !

Jack. Yes, they do sometimes ; that is, when they don't know any better.

Major. But, faith, your doorkeeper was inclined to treat me rather savagely.

Jack. That was because he did not like your face.

Major (*annoyed*). Ah, I see ; a bit of pleasantry. But may I ask if I am addressing Mr. Noel Blake ?

Jack. No, you have not the mentioned pleasure. My name is Jack Brandt.

Madge. Mr. Blake lives here, but at present is not at home. We will receive for him any message you might care to leave.

Major. Thanks ; but if you will allow me, I would rather await his return.

Jack. Well, you have my permission.

> [*As* MADGE *places chair for him,* MAJOR *raises glass to his eye ; looks her over.*

Major. Thanks. (*Aside.*) These Bohemians are certainly not the best bred people in the world. Thanks, my dear. (*To* MADGE.) By Jove, the girl is a beauty. I wonder what she is doing here. Ah, a model, I suppose.

Madge (*runs to door*). Oh, I believe I hear Noel's step upon the stair now. Ah, yes, and here he is. (**Enter** NOEL, L. C.) Noel, this gentlemen is waiting to see you.

Noel. Whom have I the honor of addressing?

Major (*rising ; presents his card*). Major Wrangle, at your service. I called to see you on a little matter of business connected with your profession. I suppose you have in your collection of music a requiem or a *de profundis*—something, in short, of a melancholy description.

Noel. Certainly. An unrecognized composer is sure to have his hands full of attempts in every style. But may I ask to what I am indebted for the honor of this visit?

[*Crosses to piano for music.*

Major. I am one of the few relatives of the late Wm. Gale.

Jack (*rising and crossing* C.). Oh, yes, the musical amateur whose death you were reading about this morning, Noel.

Major. The same, sir. Music was his all-absorbing passion ; and just before he died he expressed a desire to have one of your compositions performed at his funeral. I always make it a point to gratify the caprice of a dying man.

Noel (*giving music*). Then, sir, as a token of gratitude to my solitary admirer, allow me to present you with what you came here to purchase.

Major. My dear Blake, I couldn't think of it ; business is business, you know.

Jack (*crossing*). Correct ; business is business, and that march (*taking music from* NOEL) will cost you fifty dollars.

Major (*drawing out money*). Very well.

Noel (*taking music from* JACK). Jack, what do you mean? Put up your money, sir ; I do not want it, and this will answer all requirements. [*Gives music.*

Major. But, my dear sir, there is enough here for twenty funerals.

Noel. It's the band parts that make it appear so bulky.

Major (*aside*). I breathe again.

Jack (*crossing*). I am glad to hear it. The room is a little close, but you will find more air on the outside. (*Opens door.*) Good-morning.

Major (*going up*). Ah, to be sure. Good-morning.

[**Exit** L. C.

Noel. Was there ever anything to equal the insolence of those rich people?

Jack. Nothing ; unless it might be the false pride of some

poor people. But let it go ; we have something more important
to talk about. [*Racket of dog barking and women
screaming outside.*

Enter BLANCHE *and* MRS. VAN SLICK.

Mrs. V. S. Oh, what a horrid brute. A very formidable
animal, sir, a horrid animal.

Blanche (*laughing*). Very, and he made you jump so,
mamma ; I couldn't help laughing. I was so afraid all your
back hair would tumble down. Didn't he, mamma ?

Mrs. V. S. My dear baby, please do be quiet. Is Mr. Noel
Blake here ?

Noel. At your service, madam.

Mrs. V. S. I presume, Mr. Blake, that you have something
of a weird, crawly nature amongst your musical odds and
ends—a requiem, or something of that sort of thing.

Jack (*coming down*). Not such a thing left, madam. We
have just disposed of the last one in stock. Now, if you could
use a nice funeral march, we can let you have one in capital
condition and on very reasonable terms.

Mrs. V. S. Is this intended for a joke, sir ?

Noel. No, madam ; but I am sorry to say that I have just
disposed of my last one a moment ago to a certain Major
Wrangle.

Mrs. V. S. (*screams*). Oh, the wretch ! He knew I was
coming here, and so has forestalled me. But I will not be
beaten ; and so as you have not got a requiem, I must be satisfied with the funeral march your friend here has mentioned.
And as I cannot think of bargaining with an artist of your
merit, if you will kindly name your price——

Noel. I certainly cannot ask you to pay for what I offered to
Major Wrangle for nothing.

Mrs. V. S. You are very kind, but you will at least allow
me in return to present your sister here with a slight token in
recognition of your kindness to me, will you not ?

Noel (*going* L.). Certainly. [**Exit** L.

Blanche (*who has been all this time looking around studio
and talking to* MADGE, *comes and looks over* JACK'S *shoulder,
where he is working all the time at easel*). Oh, mamma,
come here quick. Look ! Why, it is Uncle William's picture
he is painting, isn't it, mamma ?

Mrs. V. S. (*crossing and examining picture*). Why, so it
is ; and what a splendid likeness !

Jack. Ha, ha ! So Mr. Wm. Gale was our noble stranger,
was he ? I now begin to understand.

Mrs. V. S. Surely you were not painting his portrait without
knowing his name ? There must be a story connected with such
a strange affair.

2

Madge. Indeed there is, and one that we are all proud of, too.

Blanche. Oh, please tell it to me, do. I just dote upon stories, don't I, mamma ?

Mrs. V. S. My dear baby, don't be so indiscreet. Young lady, if there is a little romance connected with my poor deceased relative and that picture yonder, we would be pleased to hear it. We are all attention.

Madge. Well, ma'am, we were all—Jack, Noel, and myself —sitting in this room one evening about a week ago. Noel had just completed his symphony and I was running it over on the piano with him, when, just as the last bars were reached, the door opened softly and a dark figure stepped in, and stood in the shadow silent as the grave.

Jack (*turning around*). Old and wrinkled, face like a piece of parchment Moses might have used, nose like an eagle's beak, an ivory-headed cane in his hand, and a cameo ring upon his little finger.

Blanche (*clapping hands*). Oh, that is Uncle William exactly. How clever you are, isn't he, mamma ?

Mrs. V. S. My dear baby !

Madge. Well, just as the last notes died away, he came forward, and, begging our pardon, excused himself by saying that he was passing by when the music arrested his attention. And could we tell him the name of the composer of the piece that we had just finished playing—that it was worthy of a Beethoven.

Jack. "Well," I replied, coming forward as proud as a peacock, "the composer of the symphony that you have just been listening to is my friend Mr. Noel Blake." With that, the old man asked Noel and Madge to play it over once more, and, after they had complied with his request, he went up to Noel, and patting his shoulder, said, in tones of remarkable sweetness, "Mr. Blake, you are a master," and you can bet your sweet life he knew what he was talking about, too.

Madge. And then he sat down and asked us about ourselves, our mode of living, and our ambitions, in such a kind, fatherly way, that we just told him everything.

Jack. And when he was going, he said to me, "Mr. Brandt, I want you to paint me a picture that will remind me of this scene and of this night in after years ; for here to-night in this room I have spent the happiest hour of my whole life." And placing a roll of money in my hand, simply saying, "Accept this on account," he vanished before we thought to ask his name.

Madge. That is all, ma'am, and we have never seen him since.

Blanche. What an interesting story, and how well they told it, didn't they, mamma ?

Enter NOEL *from* L., *with music.*

Noel. Here is the music, madam, and I hope it will please you.

Mrs. V. S. There is no doubt but what it will ; and, my dear child, your story has interested me very much. Rest assured I will not forget your kindness to my poor deceased relative. You will not refuse the bestowal of a slight token, will you ?

Madge. I will accept it gladly in my cousin's name and Jack's as in my own.

Mrs. V. S. Your cousin's name ? Then this, Mr. —— (*points to* JACK), is your brother, I suppose ?

Madge. Oh, no ; Jack is no relative at all. But I have lived with him all of my life nearly.

Mrs. V. S. (*horrified ; aside*). Oh dear, what shocking immorality. (*To* BLANCHE, *who has been flirting with* NOEL.) Baby, come to me this instant. (JACK *rises and is going to escort her out.*) Thanks, but you need not disturb yourself. Young girl, if you will please follow me to my carriage, I will give you the present I spoke of. Come, baby. Oh, what immorality ! [**Exit** L. C.; NOEL *sees them out, then comes down.*

Noel. Jack, there goes a most charming woman. And what a lovely girl !

Jack. Yes ; but did you notice how stiff your charming woman got all of a sudden when she found out in what relation we both stood toward Madge ?

Enter MADGE.

Madge. Oh, Jack, see what she has given me. I don't like to open it, for it is such fun guessing. Now, you guess first.

Jack. Well, Madge, I think that Mrs. Van Slick's present looks very much like money.

Noel. Money ! Why, the thought is absurd !

Madge. Well, here goes to find out. (*Opens packet.*) Yes, Jack is right ; see—a note and some gold.

Noel. Why, this is a greater outrage than the major's. I will throw it into the street. [*Business of* JACK *and* NOEL.

Jack. Hold on, lad. No more expensive treats to-day. The exchequer won't stand it, and you must remember she does not understand the circumstances of our little household and is obliged to judge from appearances.

Madge. · Jack, what do you mean ?

Jack. Nothing that you would understand. And now for my important subject. Noel, you lucky dog, Madge loves you.

Madge. Oh, Jack !

Jack. And, Madge, it is you whom Noel feels so wretched bout. I was a brute to talk to you in the riddle I did a short while ago.

Madge. Noel, is this true?

Noel. Haven't you just heard Jack say so?

Jack. And now, Madge, let me advise you to look to your tucks and furbelows, for you are to be married in a month's time. [*Voice outside: "Letter for you." A letter is thrown in at door; NOEL picks it up.*

Jack. Hello! what is this? Another order for a requiem, old man? You had better get a lot of those things in stock.

Noel (*reads*). "Sir: In accordance with the desire of my late client, William Gale, I have the pleasure to inform you that, with the exception of a small legacy of three thousand dollars a year left to your artist friend, Mr. Jack Brandt, you are the sole heir to his vast fortune. Your presence, with that of your cousin and your friend, Mr. Brandt, is requested at the reading of the last will and testament of the deceased at his late residence at Woodlawn, on Tuesday morning, the 16th, at 10 A. M. We have, sir, the honor of being your humble servants, RABBET & SMALL, Attorneys-at-Law." Jack, what does it all mean?

Jack. Well, old man, it means that you have made a ten-strike and tumbled into luck clear up to your eyes. It means that at last your dream of wealth is about to be realized. And, by Jove, Miss Madge, don't you think it comes just in the nick of time? You will now be able to have a very swell honeymoon.

Noel. On Tuesday, the 16th, at 10 A. M. I suppose we will meet our visitors of to-day there also.

Jack. Without a doubt. And you will also have the satisfaction of hearing your music properly performed. And now we will have to look alive, for we have hardly time to make the proper preparations for our visit. [*All going.*

Madge. But stay, Jack. We are going out of our little humble home into a new world. Oh, Jack, what if we are leaving all of our happiness behind?

Jack. Nonsense, child. And, if we are—well, we shall know where it is, at least, and we can come back here again to find it.

CURTAIN.

ACT II.

Scene.—*Garden or park at Woodlawn; Hudson River at back; rustic benches, etc. JACK BRANDT discovered R. 1 E., sketching; VAN lying at his feet. If a set house is used on L., all entrances and exits from that side can be made through house.*

Jack. Scarcely three short months since he has become a rich man, and in that short time such changes have taken place

in his tastes and desires that I sometimes wonder if it can be
the same ambitious, impatient lad who lived in the old garret
over there in New York—at war with the public because it
would not come and do homage to his art.   His art !   Why, the
word is a stranger to him now—all of his time and thoughts are
given up to pleasure—lawn parties, tennis, rowing, fishing, and
Heaven knows what else, while the art that he professed once to
love so much lies idle and neglected.   And there is Madge, too.
Poor little Madge !   Sometimes·I think I can discover a change
there, too ; but she still meets him with the same sweet, win-
some smile, and seems not to notice that she no longer holds
him in her train as of old, or that the person of that little baby-
faced Miss Van Slick has more charms for him than poor Madge
ever had.   (*Sighs*.)   What if the words she uttered as we left
the old home, that we might be leaving all of our happiness
behind us, should be prophetic after all.   (*Looks towards
house*, L.)   Ah, here comes the Major and her highness Mrs.
Van Slick.   So, Van, my boy, we had better make ourselves
scarce until after her majesty has taken her constitutional.
                              [**Exit** R. 1 E. *with* VAN.

Enter MAJOR *and* MRS. VAN, L. 1 E.

Mrs. V. S.   Oh, what a smell !   That horrid artist, Mr.
Brandt, has been out here with his more horrid pipe.   It is
really too bad that poor Mr. Blake has to put up with the presence of that vile wretch.   And only think, Major, only yesterday I found that horrid dog of his asleep upon upon one of the
new Turkish divans in the drawing-room.   Can nothing be
done, Major, to rid us of this intolerable nuisance ?   You seem
to have a very great influence over Mr. Blake.   Now, my dear
Major, cannot something be done ?

Major.   Well, Mrs. Van Slick, I promise you to talk with
Blake about the matter.   But you intimated to me, when you
proposed this meeting yesterday, that you had a more important
matter to broach to me.

Mrs. V. S.   True, Major ; you see, I have not got over
the surprise that the disposal of my cousin's property gave me.
Of course, if you alone were the only one cut off with a shilling,
I would not have been so much put out, because he often told
me that he would never leave you anything on account of your
being such a spendthrift.   [*Sits on seat* R.

Major.   Well, really, I must say that your candor is, to say
the least, refreshing.   But still, although my departed relative
saw fit to ignore me in his will, feeling, as you say, that his
fortune would not be safe in my hands, still I say, my dear
Mrs. Van Slick, I have found a way by which a goodly sum of
that same fortune has found its way to my pocket.

Mrs. V. S.   And possessing that very knowledge is the reason of my asking you for this interview. You are aware after I found that I was not remembered in my cousin's will to any great extent, how by ingratiating myself into Mr. Blake's favor, I was invited to make my home here and to take full charge of his great estate.

Major. True ; and from the way you have handled the reins since you took them up, I see no reason for you to complain. For, my dear Mrs. Van Slick, between you and me, poor Blake has been simply a figurehead. Everything has been left to your judgment and discretion.

Mrs. V. S. Major, like yourself, I am hopelessly in debt, and having been looking forward to inheriting something at the death of my cousin to be able to free myself from the importunities of my creditors, now in my desperation I have formed a plan by which, with your aid, I can practically command the expenditures and have full control of what should rightfully have been mine.

Major. My dear Mrs. Van Slick, pray command me. What is it you propose ?

Mrs. V. S. A marriage.

Major (*whistles*). Ah ! a marriage ! And with whom, I pray ?

Mrs. V. S. Mr. Blake and Blanche, my daughter.

Major. To be sure. A very pretty scheme, and one by which, if carried out, you could find a way to control the vast fortune of your son-in-law to your own satisfaction. But, my dear, where do I come in in this little drama ?

Mrs. V. S. Help me to make Blanche Mrs. Noel Blake, and upon the day they are married I will make you a present of ten thousand dollars.

Major. But is there not some sort of an engagement existing at present between Blanche and Bertie Follet ? And is not Blake to marry his cousin Madge next month ?

Mrs. V. S. I have got him to postpone his marriage with Madge for three months on the ground, as I have pointed out to him, that society would be outraged at the want of respect which he would otherwise show to his dead benefactor. And in three months, Major, one cannot tell what may happen.

Major. True ; but this affair between Blanche and Bertie Follet——

Mrs. V. S. A mere boy and girl episode. Mr. Blake has been given to understand and look at it in that light also. Have you not noticed how very attentive he has been to Blanche of late ? I have instructed her in the part she is to play, and you can rest assured I will see that she plays it to perfection. But we must hit upon some plan to cause a rupture between Mr. Blake and his artist friend Brandt, so as to get him from the field ; for, while he remains here, I fear for the success of our plans.

Major. My dear Mrs. Van Slick, I will enter heartily into your scheme to help you to a rich son-in-law ; for, I confess, since I first laid eyes upon his beautiful young cousin, I have had serious thoughts in that direction myself.

Mrs. V. S. I see ; and in joining forces with me you will be only getting a rival out of the way. (*Laughs.*) Well, as we now understand each other, my business with you is accomplished ; so let us return fo the house, as I have to get things in preparation for the ball this evening. (*As they* **exeunt** L. 3 E., *they meet* JACK *coming on from* R. 3 E. *They should meet at* C. JACK *is smoking : he lifts his hat.*) Oh, that horrid pipe !
[**Exit** L. 3 E. *with* MAJOR.

Jack (*looking after her*). A difference in taste that is, madam, I assure you. (*Sits on seat.*) I thought they had gone, else I should not have returned so soon. Now I wonder what new deviltry they have concocted for Noel's delectation ? Poor Noel ! poor lad ! He was a great deal happier in the old garret with all his pining after wealth than he is now with the dream of his life within his grasp. How like the moth is he that flutters about the flame, burning out its life, yet knowing it not. (BLANCHE *laughs* L.) The devil ! here comes that little brainless child, with her more than idiot companion, Mr. Bertie Follet. Well, like the Wandering Jew of old, I must flit for rest elsewhere. [**Exit** R. 1 E.

Enter BLANCHE *and* BERTIE *from* L. 1 E.

Blanche. No, Bertie, dear, I have no hope at all now of our ever getting married since mamma has failed in inheriting my uncle's fortune. You know that was the condition upon which she gave her consent to our engagement. And she told me only a few weeks ago that I must look upon our engagement as broken and must prepare to marry a rich husband ; and that I must try and cultivate the attention and society of Mr. Blake upon every possible occasion. Oh, Bertie, why not go to work like a man and carve out a fortune for us both ?

Bertie (*aghast*). What did you say, Miss Blanche ? Work ! Why, my dear girl, don't insult me ! Work ! Why, really, the name makes me shudder ! Please look at these hands. Why, don't you know that the Follets never did a stroke of work in all their lives ? You see your mother spoke so hopefully about her inheriting your uncle's fortune that I really saw no great risk to myself in offering you my heart, hand, and name, you know. But now I find I have been most cruelly deceived.

Blanche. Deceived, indeed ! It is I who have been deceived. I thought you loved me as you said you did, but now I find it was the money that I might inherit that you loved instead. And now, because I'm poor, you will forsake me and go out and dance attendance upon that hateful Miss Bosworth. If you loved me as I love you, we might be quite romantic and elope.

Bertie. Elope! Why, I haven't got enough to keep me in cigarettes.

Blanche. Still, you might find work at something or another. How nice living in a cottage would be, dear ; and how very romantic.

Bertie. Yes, the romantic part is all very well, but when you come to the working part, you know, my hands would get large and black and dirty, and that would never do for a Follet, you know.

Blanche (*looking off* L.). And here comes Mr. Blake, and my eyes are all red. I must not let him see them. Come, Bertie let us go for a stroll down by the lake.   [*Goes* R.

Bertie (*going* R.). Damn that Blake ! I would like to strike him quite hard. But, no ; that would be beneath the dignity of a Follet.   [**Exit** *with* BLANCHE R. 1 E.

Enter MESSENGER, *running.*

Messenger. Mr. Follet ! Mr. Follet !   [*Stands* R. 1 E.

Bertie (*entering* R. 1 E.). Did you call me, sir ?

[MESSENGER *gives dispatch.*

Bertie (*reads*). "New York, Aug. 17th. Uncle Will died this morning. Come at once.—FATHER." Uncle Will dead ! And I am his heir. Why, Blanche and I can marry now anyway and Blake be hanged !

[**Exit,** *calling,* "*Blanche ! Blanche !*"

Enter NOEL *and* MADGE, L. 3 E.

Noel. As usual, Madge, I find you making a tomboy of yourself, running around all alone by yourself. How often have I forbidden your climbing trees, and just now when I wanted you I could not find you anywhere in the house ; and when I looked for you in the grounds, instead of finding you ensconced in one of the numerous summer-houses, enriching your mind by reading some good book, where did I find you ? Perched away on the top of a great oak tree where, should you have happened to fall, it would have been instant death. I tell you, Madge, this must stop. Instead of acting like some wild creature, climbing trees and chasing butterflies, I wish you would take pattern by the beautiful and refined Miss Van Slick, and become, for the sake of the position you occupy, if for no other reason, a little more ladylike.

Madge. Don't be angry with me, dear. I did want to see those dear little chicks up there in their nest so much. I was not afraid of falling, and I knew none of your five guests would see me, because they never come to that part of the grounds. (*Putting her arms around his neck.*) Now kiss me and make up, and I promise I will try and not displease you again.

Noel (*repulses her*). Oh, never mind all that. That has nothing to do with the question. (*Looks at his watch.*) It is just four o'clock. My guests will be here in a few moments, and here you are not dressed yet.

Madge. Dressed! Why, yes, I am. This is the best one I've got, and I was careful not to tear it up in the tree. (*Sighs and sits L.*) Ah, Noel, I feel that even if I were as smart and as well dressed as Miss Van Slick, I would still be out of place amongst your fine people. [*Cries.*

Noel. Now why do you talk and act like this? And why do you look so miserable of late? You act as quiet as a mouse and keep us all at a distance.

Madge. Perhaps, Noel, it is you that keep me at a distance.

Noel. Oh, of course; it is I who am to blame for everything. Throw it all upon my shoulders. Why, Madge, can you not understand the position this fortune has placed me in? And that in order to get on in society I must make friends for myself?

Madge. And have we not good friends enough already? Why should we not send for some of our dear old friends, and let them enjoy a little of our prosperity? There is poor Warner, for instance, and the babies—they would be glad to come, and the change, I am sure, would do them good.

Noel. Oh, nonsense! That is out of the question. But I wish you would bear in mind my wishes regarding your studying the manner and graces of the Van Slicks. Cultivate their society more, for I am satisfied that if you do you will profit by their companionship.

Madge. I do try, dear, but I feel ill at ease in their presence; and, besides, I like to keep poor Jack company. He seems so out of place and lonely here.

Noel. Oh! Jack. Let Jack growl like a bear in his corner, if he chooses; but for you, I repeat, you will do well to cultivate the society of the Van Slicks.

Madge. Ah, Noel, I am afraid that the poor little orphan who knocked at your father's door one winter's night with her little bundle under her arm will never make a fine lady.

[*Rises and goes L. 1 E., crying.*

Noel. What is the matter now? And where are you going?

Madge. To my room. I do not feel well and wish to be alone.

[*Exit L. 1 E.*

Enter MAJOR, R. 3 E.

Noel. Foolish child! Thank Heaven, I have sense enough for us both.

Major. Ah, good-morning, my dear Blake. I have been looking for you everywhere. By the way, I am going to run down to the city this evening, and as I am a little short, can you oblige me by giving me a check for this I. O. U. which I got from you last evening ? It's only for a small amount—$2,000.

Noel. Why, certainly. And as I have my check-book with me, I will write it for you now. (*Business of making out check.*) There it is. But remember, to-night you must give me my revenge when you return.

Major. With pleasure, my dear boy. But was not that your little cousin I saw going as I came in ?

Noel. Yes, she has gone to her room. She is not feeling well, and I wished her to take a little rest before the festivities began this evening.

Major. Though I have not the honor of being enrolled upon the list of your cousin's particular friends, still I have always thought her a remarkably pretty girl. A diamond in the rough, as it were, needing the skill of the polisher to develop its true value. And now that the thought comes to me, I hope that there is nothing serious in the rumor I have heard regarding your marriage.

Noel. Why do you ask ?

Major. Pray forgive the seeming impertinence of my question, but the fact is I am deeply interested in your welfare, and I deem it only my duty as a friend to remind you that, while you were at liberty to marry for love and all that sort of thing when you were only a poor struggling musician, a man in your present position owes a certain duty to society, and is not, in the eyes of society, justifiable in throwing himself away.

Noel. Not if he pledged his word ?

Major. Under the circumstances—no. My dear fellow, I understand your case thoroughly. It was only a feeling of false delicacy which induced you to bind yourself to the fulfilment of a thoughtless promise, which, of course, while highly creditable to you and all that, is still wholly thrown away. My dear fellow, just take my advice : put an end to this entanglement at once, make your cousin a present of a nice little dowry with which to make some fortunate fellow happy later on, and you may, if you play your cards right (*nudges him*), you lucky dog, marry Mrs. Van Slick's daughter before the year is out.

Noel. But Miss Blanche's affections appear to be already engaged.

Major. Nothing but mere childish folly, I assure you. You can have her for the asking ; and in making her your wife you ally yourself to one of the oldest families in the country. She raises you to her level, and the doors of the best people in society will be thrown open to you. (*Looks at his watch.*) But

I must go and dress. (*Going* L.) But think it over. Oh, you lucky dog ! How I envy you your chance !   [**Exit** L. 3 E.

Enter MISS BLANCHE *from house*, L. I E.

Blanche. Bertie ! Bertie ! (*Discerns* NOEL.) Oh ! Mr. Blake ! Pray pardon me, but I thought you were Bertie—I mean, Mr. Follet.

Noel. Really, Miss Van Slick, this is a most unlooked-for pleasure. And dressed so early too ! This is a delightful surprise.

Blanche. Oh, that is what mamma did it for, and in the rush my maid ran the pins into me in a dreadful manner, so that I would be in time to meet you before the other guests arrived. And then mamma saw you out here, and told me to run out and act as though the meeting was accidental, you know. I did it well, didn't I, Mr. Blake ?

Noel. It is a pleasure, nevertheless. What a charming toilet ! I am afraid you have laid yourself open to a great many critical remarks from some of my fair guests to-day. A woman may forgive another for being prettier, but never for being better dressed.

Blanche. Oh, I'm glad you like my dress, for if you didn't it would have been an awful waste of money. Mamma said that she might as well be hung for a sheep as a lamb, and that the dressmaker's bill was so large now, that one more item wouldn't make much difference.

Enter JACK *back* R. U. E.; *listens.*

Noel. Ah, what a pleasure it would be to me to be given the right to pay all your little bills and your mother's also in the future.

Blanche. Well, I am sure mamma would feel it a great pleasure and relief also. (*Sees* JACK.) Oh, there is Mr. Brandt. I can go now, can't I, Mr. Blake ? Mamma told me only to speak with you. She did not say I was to amuse Mr. Brandt.

[NOEL *sees her off* L. I E.

Jack (*coming down* R.). And yet, my dear Miss Van Slick, you do amuse me extremely. (*Sits* R. *as* NOEL *comes up*.) Noel, my lad, you deserve a medal from the humane society, and no mistake.

Noel. What do you mean ?

Jack. I mean your daily efforts to rescue that poor brainless child for a time from her mamma's terrible clutches can only be prompted by the sublimest heroism on your part.

Noel. I find Miss Van Slick very agreeable company, and I think it would do Madge no harm, let me tell you, if she had a little of Miss Van Slick's refinement.

Jack. I am afraid you think Madge a little awkward, don't you, Noel ?

Noel. Well, a little, I must confess.

Jack. And yet the time is very short—three short months—since you felt quite otherwise.

Noel. Well, you see, my position has changed since then.

Jack. True ; but, by the way, lad, do you know the name of Madge's mother—I mean her maiden name ?

Noel. No. Father always spoke of his friend and wife as though there was some mystery about them. Why do you ask ?

Jack. Why, one of your friends met me in the park a short while ago—you know the one I mean—an old man, the one who was so struck by a resemblance he saw between Madge and some one belonging to him.

Noel. Oh, you mean old Beresford—the retired banker. His daughter ran away with some opera singer or actor, and the event, they say, has unsettled his brain. He is continually discovering a resemblance in every fresh face that he sees.

Jack. Well, he told me the reason this morning. Before his daughter died she wrote him, asking him to provide for her child, a little girl. He was to recognize her by a certain birthmark. But it seems he was travelling, and the letter never reached him for months afterwards, and when he tried to find his grandchild he was told that the father had hired a nurse and had taken her on his travels with him.

Noel. Well, I hope he will find her some time. But you must excuse me now, Jack, as I must go and prepare to receive my guests.   [*Going* L.

Jack. And I'll go for a stroll and a smoke as a sort of bracer for my plunge into society.   [*Going* R. U. E.

Noel (*turning*). Look here, Jack, do you intend to wear that suit of clothes the rest of your life ?

Jack (*coming down*). No, I'm afraid I can't, unless I die sooner than I expect to. (*Examining.*) By the looks of things now, I am afraid I will have to be ordering another in about a year or two.

Noel. Why are you so dead to what is going on around you ? Don't you see that Miss Van Slick is always making fun of you behind your back ? Why, the servants make a butt of you.

[*Crosses to* R.

Jack (*coming down* L.). Oh, your servants object to my old shooting jacket, do they ? By Jove ! it is lucky for me that they see me sometimes in the society of such a swell as their master.

Noel. And I also wish you would look after that dog of yours a little closer. You know Mrs. Van Slick is terribly afraid of him, and the other day she found him asleep in her boudoir and had hard work to drive the brute out.

Jack. Poor old Van! You see, Noel, he thinks that he is still in the old garret at home where the furniture was not too good to be used.

Noel. Well, he would be just as well off in the stables here.

Jack. Well, Noel, lad, I will see that he annoys your fine friends no more. But I couldn't think of putting him in your stable; for I am afraid that he would be putting on airs if he associated much with your servants.

Enter MADGE *from* L. 3 E., *running, dressed in a fashionable evening gown.*

Madge (*runs to* NOEL *and embraces him*). Oh, you dreadful impostor you! Now I understand the reason of the scolding you gave me a short while ago. I confess that it did make me feel a little unhappy, and I left you to go and have a good cry all alone. But when I got to my room, there was this beautiful new dress spread out on my bed, bouquet and all; and old Mrs. Kennet, beaming with smiles and ready to dress me. Look, Jack, did you ever see anything to equal it? Everything in such perfect taste. [*Business ad libitum.*

Noel. But I don't understand. What do you mean?

Madge. Oh, of course not. But you are not going to deceive me again, sir, I can tell you. (*Goes to him.*) Dear Noel, you have made me so happy; you have no idea what all your thoughtful kindness means to me at this time. I was beginning to think——

Noel (*repulsing her*). But I tell you again I don't understand. There is some mistake. Of course, if I knew that you wanted a dress, I should have been pleased to have given you one; but it really never occurred to me.

Madge (*surprised*). Then this is not your present, nor the money Mrs. Kennet has given to me from time to time.

Noel (*crossing to* L.). I tell you I know nothing about it; and now please excuse me, as I have a great many things to look after for the entertainment of my guests this afternoon.

[**Exit** L. 1 E.

Madge. And I was so happy! Yet he never gave me a thought. (*Looks at* JACK; *starts; then goes over slowly to him* L.) Thank you, Jack. And please forgive me for not understanding before. [*Turns from him and weeps.*

Jack. What is this? Tears! Why, child, all the dresses in New York are not worth such thanks as these. But you see, Madge, it is just as Noel says,—he did not think. So I——

Madge. I understand Only, Jack, you did not wait to be asked. Oh, Jack, take away from this place, where we have both stayed too lo ly. Let us go back to the dear old room, where, if w njoy the splendor that surrounds us here, we can at le e happy together.

Jack. Why, you silly little woman, what do you think Noel would say to that? You must not think of such a thing, for the sake of your own happiness.

Madge. My happiness! Where is it? Has it not been slipping away from me day by day, hour by hour, from the moment I first came here? No, Jack, you feel as I do, though you will not admit it, that my poor little dream is over, and Noel will soon begin to be ashamed of me, as he is already of his art and his old friends.

[*Kisses his hands and* **exit** *quickly,* L. I E.

Jack (*looking after her*). Madge! (*Calls.*) Gone; and she kissed my hands! And as her tears fell upon them, they seemed to burn, and made me feel as though I had been stung. (*Sighs.*) Poor child! How she loves him; and that miserable fellow throws away like a withered leaf a love that would make the best and brightest joy of another's life.

[**Exit** R. I E. *slowly. Singing and laughter heard at back. Then* **enter** DALE, SMILEY, *and others* R. 3 E. *This part can be played ad libitum up to the entrance of* JACK.

Dale. Bring along the hampers, boys. This is a glorious sport. And hurry and get out the viands, for that sail down the river has made me as hungry as a bear.

[*Table is spread on the grass ; business of getting ready and eating during the following speeches.*

Smiley. I say, Dale, isn't Blake's summer residence somewhere around here on the river?

Dale. So it is, old chappie. Joe Smith wrote me that it was near Tarrytown. By Jove, old boy, what do you say to hunting him up after we have had our lunch?

Smiley. A capital idea! He will be delighted to see us, no doubt. And I am just dying for a sight of dear old Jack and little Madge.

Dale. I say, Smiley, Madge struck a snap after all when she caught Noel.

Smiley. Oh, I don't know. I'm willing to bet now that she has the worst end of the bargain.

Enter JACK, R. I E.

Jack. Gentlemen, are you aware—— (*Surprised.*) What, Smiley! Dale! Well, old boys, I am delighted.

Dale *and* **Smiley.** The happiness is mutual, old chap.

Dale. In fact, we were just speaking about you.

Smiley. But I say, Jack, where are Madge and Noel? We are just dying for a sight of them.

Dale. Jack, allow me to introduce you the members of the Bohemian Club, just out for a pleasure. Feeling the calls of the inner man a little too strong to resist any longer, we concluded to stop here and satisfy his cravings. Please squat right down and join us. But first, what is the name of this Arcadian vale ?

Jack. This is Woodlawn, the summer home of Noel Blake, Esquire.

Smiley *and* **Dale.** Hip ! hip ! hurrah ! Port at last !

Jack. And here comes Madge now to speak for herself.

Madge (*running*). Oh, Jack ! (*Discerns party.*) What, my dear old friends, Dale and Smiley ! This is indeed a pleasure.

Dale. Little Madge now blossomed into a fashionable young lady.

Madge. Yes, little Madge, who now having you here will not let you leave in a hurry, I can tell you.

Dale. Generous girl ! And these are the members of the Bohemian Club—you remember the name of our new musical comedy I wrote you about.

Madge. Oh, I remember ; and how did you succeed ?

Smiley. Capitally. The skit made a positive hit. Oh, by-the-by, you never heard the score of it, did you ? Well, as we are here, we will, with your permission, run through the first act. [*Business ad libitum. An act from some musical farce or comedy can be introduced.*

Madge (*at close, clapping her hands*). Bravo ! bravo !

Dale. I say, Jack, the heat is positively tropical. Oblige us by leading us to the nearest fountain and leaving us in it.

Madge (*laughs*). We have not got a fountain handy, and besides in that gorgeous dress you might frighten the fishes. But what do you say to a nice cold bottle of wine right off the ice out here under the trees in true Bohemian style ?

All. Bravo ! Capital !

Dale. Jack, will you please give the necessary orders ?

Jack. No ; on this occasion I will attend to it in person, and thus be sure of obtaining the genuine article. [**Exit** L. 3 E.

Smiley. Really, Miss Madge, had I known that you were mistress of this great domain, I would have——

Madge. Sit down there, you foolish fellows, for you will find me the same Madge whom you used to dance upon your knee, and who has so often lit that old, familiar pipe you are endeavoring so hard to hide from my gaze. Come, let me light it for you now, just to show you I have not forgotten the art. (*All the men produce pipes, the girls cigarettes, and smoke.*) There ! the smell of that old pipe is far sweeter to my nostrils than all Miss Van Slick's fine perfume.

Enter *from* L. I E. MRS. VAN SLICK, BLANCHE, *and* MAJOR.

Mrs. Van Slick (*coughing*). What a horrible smell of

tobacco! (*Discovers party up back*.) Oh, goodness gracious! Major, just look there! (**Enter** NOEL, L. 1 E.) How came they on the grounds? (NOEL *crosses over to* MRS. V. S., R.) And, as I live, Miss Madge is amongst them! I suppose, my dear Noel, this is another of Mr. Jack Brandt's graceful jests. (JACK **enters** *from* L. *with bottles*.) It is not enough that ladies are to be terrified out of their lives by his very formidable dog, but now they must be poisoned by his friends' vile-smelling tobacco, not to speak of the insult offered to us by their vulgar practice.

Noel. Allow me, my dear Mrs. Van Slick, to apologize for their presence in his name, and to assure you that his dog, his friends, or anything connected with him will not annoy you after to-day.

Major. Spoken like a true gentleman, sir; damn me if it ain't. [*Business of bowing to the ladies.*

Noel (*crossing over to party*). Mr. Dale and Mr. Smiley, I believe.

Madge. Yes, Noel, our old friends. Isn't it just jolly to have them with us again?

Noel. I am sorry, Madge, I cannot enter into your enjoyment of meeting your friends, as you are pleased to term them. And, owing to the fact that my house is quite full of guests at present, I am sorry that I cannot ask for the pleasure of their further company. I shall be happy to place my carriage at their disposal. (*Looking at his watch.*) By starting at once, they will be able to reach the station in time to catch the next train for New York.

Madge. Noel, are you mad? Why, these are our old and true friends—Jack's guests.

Noel. When Mr. Jack Brandt has a home of his own I shall not question his choice of friends. I claim only the same privilege here, where I am the master. [MADGE **exit** L. 2 E.

Smiley. Will some one pinch me? Was it Noel Blake I heard speak those words—and to us?

Jack (*coming forward*). Forget them, friends. Forget them and the cur who dared give such words utterance. He wishes, it seems to me, to break with all of his old friends. He is a wealthy man now, and it is beneath his dignity to associate with his old Bohemian set. He has insulted you, Smiley—you who sold the coat from off your own back only a short time ago in order to purchase wine for him when he lay sick with fever.

Noel. Brandt, do you wish to humiliate me by recalling the past?

Jack. No; I merely wished to remind you of it. You seem to have forgotten so much already that should have been sacred to you. I know that I am a rough sort of a fellow, and that my appearance here in my shabby coat is like a blot upon your splendor, and I am now about to remove it forever from your gaze. But before I go there is one thing I wish to speak to you about. It is of Madge. Noel, be true to her, treat her kindly, and give to her the love that her tender heart craves, and which I am afraid you are letting go out from you to another. This is all I ask. Grant me this last request, and I will go out into the great world and back to my old life, and will mar your prosperity no more.

Noel. Well, if what goes on here does not please you, why, you have the remedy in your own hands.

Jack (*aside*). My God ! After all my sacrifices, has it come to this ? I have the remedy in my own hands !

[*Gun fired outside ;* MADGE *runs on to* JACK.

Madge. Jack ! Jack ! [*Sobs in his arms.*

Jack. Madge ! what is the matter ? What has happened ?

Enter SERVANT, L. I E., *with gun.*

Madge. Oh, Jack, didn't you hear the shot ? They have killed poor Van.

Jack. What ! Killed my faithful dog—my only true friend ? (*Going to* SERVANT.) Tell me, was it you who fired that shot ?

Servant. Yes, sir ; by the master's orders.

Jack. Noel, tell me that this fellow lies. Tell me that, at least, it was not by your orders that the cowardly deed was committed.

Noel. Well, it was by my orders that the brute was killed ; what of it ? [**Exit** SERVANT, L. I E.

Jack. You have shot Van through his faithful heart. Poor fellow ! He was good for nothing else but to love you, but like his master he humbled your magnificence by his shabby presence. [*Sinks on seat,* R.

Madge. Don't grieve, Jack ; but come with me. They will only sneer at your grief here.

Jack (*starting up*). It is not only for the dog I grieve, for it is not he alone that he is dead. The friendship that has filled my life has been murdered by the same foul blow. (*Advances.*) But the veil is torn away at last, and I can look away down to the bottom of your shallow soul and see that you are only a selfish, ungrateful coward.

Noel. Brandt !

Jack. Silence ! I have, with the true Bohemian spirit, fed you with my bread. My hopes, as you well know, were all centred in you. I even made of my talents a ladder for your genius to climb upon. If you had asked me for my life's blood, I believe I would not have denied you. And how have you rewarded me in return ? May Heaven forgive you, Noel Blake,

for you have reduced me to the infinite baseness of flinging my
own benefits in your teeth ; you have robbed me of your glory,
which was to be the end and consolation of all my sacrifices.
I had nothing left but my poor, faithful Van, and you have even
deprived me of his companionship.   You shot him that you
might be rid of his master.   Well, you have gained your point.
From this moment we are strangers.

Madge (*as* JACK *goes up*).   Jack ! Jack !   Take me with you !

Noel (*stepping* C.).   Madge !   I forbid you to stir one step.

Madge.   Don't dare to touch me, you coward !

CURTAIN.

SMILEY.

DALE.

COMPANY.

BLANCHE   JACK.

MRS. V. S.

MAJOR.

MADGE.

NOEL.

ACT III.

Scene.—*Same as Act I. ; two years supposed to have elapsed.*

Jack (**enters** *slowly*).   Well, here I am, home once more
after two years of wandering in the vain attempt to stifle the
great ever-gnawing pain at my heart.   Home once more to try
and begin the old life again.   Ah ! but with what a difference.
To think that where, a few years back, by this hearth, I had
hope, love, and friendship with me, I must henceforth sit
alone and smoke my solitary pipe.   (*Crosses to* L. *and looks at
picture on the wall.*)   And there still hangs my great inspira-
tion—the dream of my life.   How often have I longed in the old
days for the time when it should be finished.   Shall I ever have
the courage again, I wonder, to go on with it ?   Can I ever
hope to renew the colors with which it was begun—the colors
blended in such magic tints by youth, eager longing, and ambi-
tion.   (*Sighs ; turns and goes* R. *to basket.*)   As well try and
bring back my old careless self of two years ago.   And here is
little Madge's work-basket.   (*Bows his head over it for a moment before his speech, which is given in a broken voice.*)
Here is where she used to sit, so busy and so bright, where I
shall never see her sit again.   Never again shall I turn from my
easel to watch the little figure in her neat gray gown, flitting

about the room, the kindly spirit of our bachelor fireside. Poor child ! I wonder how she has prospered in the last two years. Married, no doubt, to Noel, and happy in the love of husband and children, while I—— [*Sinks into chair at table and bows his head.*

Enter FREDDIE SPROUL, L. C.; *starts, then comes down.*

Fred. What ? No ! Yes, it is ! Old Jack come back. (*Shakes his hand.*) Delighted to see you, old chap, I am, upon my word. I thought I saw some one moving around over here, so I says to Mrs. Sproul——

Jack. Mrs. Sproul ?

Fred. Yes, Mrs. Sproul, Jack ; I'm married, you know, and have got the handsomest baby, Jack, you ever saw. And, by Jove ! now that you have returned again, you must paint its portrait. Weighed sixteen pounds when it was born. Well, as I was telling you, I says to Mrs. Sproul, " I'll bet a little that is old Jack over there in the studio." Our lodgings, you see, are right across the way, so over I came to find out. By Jove ! you don't know how good it seems to have you back once more. And Miss Madge—is she with you ?

Jack. No, Freddie, I am by myself.

Fred. Oh, I see. You have just run up to see that the old place had not moved away in your absence. When are you going back ?

Jack. Never ; I have parted from Noel forever.

Fred. Parted from Noel forever ?

Jack. Yes. Did not Dale or Smiley tell you ?

Fred. I was away in Italy, I guess, when they were here, and have seen no one of the old party until this moment. But, Jack, surely you and Noel have not quarrelled ?

Jack. Yes, such is the truth. We are to each other as strangers. It is too long and wretched a story to tell you now, but some day——

Fred. Never mind about it. I am sure you were not to blame, whatever the trouble may be. But I say, Jack, come over to my rooms, and be introduced to Mrs. Sproul and that young sixteen-pounder I just told you about. He is a peach, I tell you ; and besides, you can enjoy an old time pipe with me over a little beer. What do you say ?

Jack. Thanks, my lad, for your kindness. I will accept your offer, for I must confess I feel the need of a little stimulant keenly. [**Exeunt** R. I E.

Enter MRS. KENNET, L. C.; *looks in, then enters cautiously.*

Mrs. K. Come right in, Miss Madge ; there is no one here.

Enter MADGE, *fashionably dressed.*

Mrs. K. Dear, dear, Miss, what a queer place this is, and (*snuffing*) how musty everything smells.

Madge. Yes, dear old Kennet, you see that is because it has been shut up for over two years,—years that have seemed to me like ages, but you cannot imagine how delighted I am to get back in the dear old place once more. We were so contented, Mrs. Kennet, even though we were very poor.

Mrs. K. Indeed, my dear, money does not always bring happiness. (MADGE *removes her things.*) But surely, Miss Madge, you do not mean to stop here.

Madge. Oh, no, you dear old Kennet. Grandpa has taken a suite at the Kremlin during our stay here. But I could not help coming to see the old home and Jack—I mean Mr. Brandt—for I fear that he is unhappy. Every one has seemed so unkind to him.

Mrs. K. Then, indeed, that is what Mr. Brandt don't deserve.

Madge. And least of all from me, who should have known how to read that noblest, tenderest of hearts. But, Kennet, if he should come in, you don't think that he will misjudge the cause of my presence here, do you?

Mrs. K. Why, certainly not, my dear. If he is in trouble, where else should you go but here?

Madge. Oh, thanks, and now let us put the place in order, for it needs it badly. (*Business.*) But,—oh, see,—his great picture. Oh, just help me lift it down and put it on that easel. (*Business of removing picture from easel and putting the other in its place; dusts it off.*) There, see how the colors glow, now that the dust is removed, and it has been months and months since a brush was put on it—months (*sadly*) of patient self-denial and devotion, of loneliness and misjudged affection. Forgive me, Jack! I was blind—I did not know.

[*Bows head on picture.*

Mrs. K. Come, my dear, you must not fret; that will be all over now, and Mr. Brandt will yet be as happy and as famous as no doubt he deserves to be.

Madge. Yes. We will never misunderstand him again.

Enter FRED., *running,* R. 1 E.; *stops suddenly.*

Fred. Bless me! if it isn't Miss Madge herself! (*Advancing and offering his hand.*) Well, you can't imagine how pleased I am to see you once more. And my! won't Jack be delighted?

Madge. Oh, Fred, where is he?

Fred. Right across the way at my lodging with Mrs. Sproul and the sixteen-pounder. Why, he only returned here after two years' absence a few moments ago, and I just ran over for his

pipe. Oh, Lord bless you! it seems just like old times to see
you back again. But I must run and inform Jack.

[*Going* R. I E., MADGE *catches him.*

Madge. Wait one moment, Freddie, and tell me how he is
looking. Is he well and happy?

Fred. Well, he looks as well as a man can look who has
been an inmate of a French hospital for a year.

Madge. Then he has been sick—perhaps dying.

Fred. Well, not quite so bad as that. In trying to rescue
two children from a burning building, he nearly lost the sight of
both his eyes. But, thanks to the skill of the physicians, he is all
right again. And as for happiness—— Well, Miss Madge, he
has told me about the quarrel with Noel, and I don't think that he
has quite recovered from the blow yet. But I must go and tell
him you are here. I am sure it will bring back the old life to
him again. [*Going; she catches him.*

Madge. Please don't say anything about my being here. In
fact, Dale, Smiley, and other of his old friends have just arrived
in New York from Australia, where we have been travelling,
and we are all going to meet here to-night and give him a surprise. But, Freddie, just go back and tell him you could not
find the dear old pipe, and prevail upon him to come and find
it for himself. You understand?

Fred. By Jove! An excellent plan. (*Going.*) But, Miss
Madge, don't fail to return with him to our lodgings. I wish
you to become acquainted with Mrs. Sproul and that sixteen
pounder. I tell you, he is a peach. [**Exit** R. I E.

Madge. And now, Mrs. Kennet, I will just change this costume for one that Jack will understand much better.

[**Exit** L. 3 E.

Mrs. K. Bless her dear heart! I wonder if she thinks she
can fool poor old Kennet. Don't I see that she is just a-dying
with love for Mr. Brandt? Well, I guess everything will come
out all right now; but she don't wish Mr. Brandt to know that
she is the rich granddaughter of Mr. Beresford; that is what
I can't understand. But I must get the tea ready, for I am
willing to bet that Mr. Brandt has not had a cup of decent tea
since he left Woodlawn two years ago. And well do I remember it's many a time when he would drop in to see us servants
in the kitchen, and treat us just as polite as though we were
some great ladies. And when I offered him a cup of tea, he
would say after taking a sup and holding his cup aloft in this
manner, "Kennet," he would say, "this is a necktie fit for the
gods."

Enter MADGE, L. 3 E.

Madge (*wearing dress of Act I.*). There, Kennet, how do I
look? He can come now as soon as he likes.

Mrs. K. Will I light the lamp, Miss Madge?

Madge. No, Kennet, it will be easier for me to speak to him in the dark.

Mrs. K. Very well, Miss; I will go and prepare a little lunch for you both. For you know you have not broken your fast since this morning.   [**Exit** R. 3 E.

Madge. But now what am I to say? Now that the time has come, my courage fails me. Oh, I fear I have been rash in coming here in this manner. Better that Jack should never know what I have come here to tell him, than I should sink one hairsbreath in the estimation his little Madge of the old days holds in his thoughts. (*Starts.*) There is a step on the stairs now. (*Goes to door* C.) How slow and dull and listless it sounds! [*Comes down and sits at work-basket, darning stockings.*

Enter JACK, L. C.

Jack (*surprised*). I beg your pardon, Miss, I made a mistake, my room must be on the other side.

Madge. Come right in—it's no mistake, Jack.   [*Turns.*

Jack (*gladly; rushing to her.*) What, Madge! Little Madge!   [*Staggers and drops with his head in her lap.*

Jack. Oh, Madge! is it really you, child? And what are you doing here?

Madge. Darning the stockings, Jack. And see—they need it badly.

Jack (*rising*). Yes, it is herself. Oh, child, you have come back to brighten my poor home and life once more, and in your pretty gray gown of the old days, too. (*Looking around.*) And, you little witch, you have been using your wand about the room already.

Madge. Only a broomstick, Jack; that, you know, is the proper thing for a witch.

Jack. Are you sure this is not all a dream? Madge, dear, have we really been away all this long dreary time?

Madge (*rises and gets blouse; then takes off his coat and puts blouse on instead*). I am sure you have been away somewhere, sir, to learn such extravagant habits. Are you going to wear that fine new coat in the house? That beautiful coat that you have had only five years.

Jack (*submitting to the change*). Yes; it is herself, the little Madge of old, come back to scold me and keep everything in order. (*Brightening up.*) There, madam, I hope you are satisfied now. And perhaps you will tell me the meaning of this delightful apparition on my hearthstone.

Madge. Why, of course. (*Rising.*) But after I have made the tea.   [*Going.*

Jack (*stopping her*). The kettle is not boiling yet. But where have you been, young lady, may I ask, that you have grown so very aristocratic, and forgotten the rudiments of an art in which you used to excel.

Madge. Where I should never have gone, where no one wants me any longer, and where I will never again return.

[*Sits at table and bows her head.*

Jack. What do you mean?

Madge. I mean, Jack, that everything between Noel and myself came to an end two years ago. I left Woodlawn on the same day that you did.

Jack. Great Heavens! That it should come to this!

Madge. It is not so very bad after all. I have good friends still, and I now have my big brother Jack to look after me; and there is many a poor girl who has to go and face a cold, cruel world to earn her bread without any such consolation or support.

Jack. My poor child! And how did those little hands serve you in the contact with the world you speak of? But, why talk of your working; you can trust me, Madge, can you not?

Madge. With my life, Jack.

Jack. Then let me make it my joy to work for you and make a home for you. A home, though humble, would, at least, be your own.

Madge. Jack!

Jack. I know I am selfish to speak like this so soon; I know that the disparity in our ages should keep my tongue dumb. But the thought of you here in this great cruel city, all alone, is more than I can bear. The thought of you struggling through wind, rain, and storm, day after day, to earn the miserable pittance that will hardly keep soul and body together, of the hardships you must endure, and the insults your very beauty will subject you to—oh, Madge, the first fruits of your heart cannot be mine, I know, but I will be so patient, dear, and so content with ever so little; to be allowed to work for you, to care for you, to give to you my very best, is all I ask. And, surely, after a time, when you have proved the strength of my devotion, surely a heart so tender and true as yours will find some little love in return. And I will wait for that so patiently—so patiently, dear.

Madge. Oh, you poor, foolish old Jack, you have made a little mistake when you think I have been suffering. Instead, I have been enjoying all the pleasures a heart could desire. Ah, no, Jack, I'm afraid it is you who have been the sufferer from your contact with the cruel world you speak of.

Jack. You have left Noel and have been happy since! I don't understand.

Madge. Well, then, let me explain. After you went away from Woodlawn on that dreadful day, I wished to follow you, but Noel would not allow me to. I succeeded, however, in getting away the next morning, and went direct to our old friends Dale and Smiley. You remember how eager they always were to have me join their company. Well, I offered my services and was engaged at once. And, oh, Jack, while we were rehearsing I discovered a friend who knew my mother intimately. He was not a member of the company, but he travelled with us, and his presence made me the happiest young girl in the world.

Jack (*aside*). His presence made her the happiest girl in the world. She loves some one else.

Madge. So, you dear old Jack, instead of suffering, I have been happy and contented for the past two years, winning operatic honors in Australia as the bright particular star of Dale and Smiley's Royal Operatic Company. (*Throws her arms around his neck.*) And now——

Enter NOEL, L. C.

Noel. Just as I expected. I saw in the papers this morning that the opera company that you ran away with when you left Woodlawn had arrived in New York, and I felt in a moment where I would be able to find you.

Madge (*coldly*). I think, sir, that at least you might have spared me this.

Noel. I wish to have no words about the matter. My desire is for you to leave this place at once and return with me to Woodlawn. I am a fool, no doubt, for my pains, for a girl who is so lost to all self-respect as to follow a man to his rooms alone——   [JACK *makes movement ;* MADGE *restrains him.*

Enter MRS. KENNET, R. 3 E.

Mrs. K. You are mistaken, sir ; Miss Madge came here under my protection.   [*Curtseys.*

Noel. What ! My housekeeper in revolt, too ! Mrs. Kennet, return to your duties at once ; remember you are in my services.

Mrs. K. Beg pardon, but you have made another mistake. I have always been accustomed to work for gentlemen ; therefore I am no longer in your employ. Miss Madge, I am yours whenever you want me.

Madge. Noel, did you come here to ask me to return to Woodlawn ?

Noel. I did. It is your home, and it is my place, as your affianced husband and guardian, to protect you against evil advisers, and I command you to return home with me at once.

Madge. And I refuse. I felt long before I left your roof that I stood in the way of your social advancement in the world, and there was a time when that very knowledge caused me the bitterest pain the heart of a woman can know. But now——

[*Turns to* JACK.

Noel. Well, and now——

Madge. Now I know you, and the past is at an end forever between us. I ask nothing of you henceforth but to be allowed to go my way in peace.

Noel. Madge, don't be absurd. If any nonsensical jealousy has prompted this step, you have chosen a highly unbecoming manner of showing it. I can overlook some natural annoyance at my attentions in another quarter, but your love should have been proof against such trifles.

Madge. My love ! Noel, that girlish love by which you set so little store is cold and dead. It perished the same hour as did Jack's, your benefactor's, friendship.

Jack (*starts*). Madge ! .

Noel. You will live to repent the words you are speaking.

Madge. Never ! I only wish the whole world could hear me speak, Noel. All that I thought I loved in you existed only in him. (*Points to* JACK.) He was your heart, your enthusiasm, your only good ; and he once gone, you were as one dead. You were like a body without a soul. [NOEL *winces.*

Jack. Madge, what does this mean ?

Madge. It means, Jack, that I have learned the truth at last. Ah, how could you speak to me as you did a few moments ago ? Am I such a stone, such a senseless thing as I must seem to you ? You supplicate to me when my place should be in the dust at your feet. And, Jack, here at your feet (*kneels*) I plead to you. Take me, Jack, for it is you whom I love.

Jack (*lifting her up*). Me, Madge—you love me !

Madge. Ay, with the first warm love of my heart. The early, foolish blossoms, dear, were offered (*looks at* NOEL.) to another, 'tis true ; but they are withered now and trampled under foot, and the perfect bloom and sweetness of the ripened fruit is for you, Jack, if you will only take it.

Jack (*embracing her*). My little Madge ! My life !

Noel. A very pretty scene, indeed ; I dare not intrude upon it any longer. In coming here I merely wished to prove to my own satisfaction that certain suspicions were correct before I returned to the happiness that awaits me in another quarter.

Jack. Then they have sold that poor girl to you at last, and, like the cur you are, you came here with a lie upon your lips to insult your cousin with a profession of your constancy. Well, be kind to that poor child, for, to do her justice, I am satisfied that she is an unwilling victim to the barter.

Enter MAJOR, L. C., *quickly.*

Major. My dear Blake! What the devil are you doing here? The enemy has surprised our camp and stolen the prize.

Noel. What do you mean?

Major. Just what I say. You know the wedding finery arrived yesterday from Paris. Well, to-day the wedding finery and the prize are both gone. You had the game well in hand, but at the critical moment you throw up your cards and allow Bertie Follet to step in and rake the board and bolt with her.

Noel. Bolt with whom?

Major. Damn it, man, whom else could it be but with Blanche—Miss Van Slick? A dispatch just received states they were married this morning and sail this evening for Europe. I am going now to try and head them off.   [**Exit** MAJOR, L. C.

Jack. You seem to be rather unlucky in your love affairs.

Enter BERESFORD *and* DALE, L. C.

Noel. But having plenty of money at my command, I can purchase consolation, never fear. And that reminds me. (*Draws out check-book and writes.*) As your guardian, it is my duty to see that you will not starve.   [*Offers check.*

Jack. Put up your check, sir. My promised wife has but one answer to make. It is the same you gave to your new friend, Major Wrangle, in this very room two short years ago. "Was there ever anything to equal the insolence of those rich people?"

Beresford. And allow me to add, my friend, that, being Miss Madge's grandfather, I have assumed all legal rights to her in the future.   [*Business of* DALE, JACK *and* MADGE.

Noel. You, Mr. Beresford!

Beresford. Yes, I. The proofs are ready for your inspection at any time you may wish to inspect them.

Noel. This is really an agreeable surprise. Miss Madge, allow me to congratulate you; and, really, Mr. Brandt, it is too bad that the felicity of this Arcadian scene cannot be perfected by the presence of your much-lamented dog, Van, to offer congratulations.

[*Going; door* L. C. *opens;* FREDDIE *and* SMILEY *rush in with dog and knock him over* R. *down stage, where his hat rolls off; he stands brushing his clothes until he is shown out.*

Freddie. Thanks! And here is old Van, sound and as good as new. We met the Major on our way here, and hang me if he didn't try to bite his legs.

Jack (*who has embraced the dog*). Old Van alive! Dale, how did it happen?

Dale. We had to return to the park for something we had left behind us, and Smiley found him in some shrubbery near the river, where they had flung him. Finding him not quite dead, we brought him away with us, and he has been Miss Madge's constant companion for the last two years.

Jack (*to* MADGE). And you never told me this!

Madge. No, I wished it for another surprise.

Enter SMILEY *with his arms full; also* BERTIE FOLLET *and* BLANCHE, *loaded with bundles.*

Smiley. Here I am, Dale, old chap; and I've seen Warner and all our old chums, and got all the articles you named, and had to call in aid to transport them here in the presence of Mr. and Mrs. Bertie Follet. They were, so Mr. Follet assured me, about to partake of a wedding feast, so I just brought them here where it could be enjoyed in true Bohemian style.

Noel. Blanche!

Blanche. Oh, Bertie, there is Mr. Blake.

Bertie. Oh, damn Blake! He ain't in it any more, you know; I have euchred him. (SMILEY *crosses to door* L. C.) Ah, so it is—Mr. Noel Blake. Well, Mr. Blake, as you have no doubt overheard what I have just said, and as our expected company are all toilers in the world of art, commonly called Bohemians, I am sorry that we cannot ask for your delightful company to grace our festive board.

[*Opens door and points off;* NOEL *goes up and out; shakes his fist as he* **exit.**

Jack (*to* MADGE, *while others busy themselves getting everything in readiness for the supper*). And you do not regret your choice? Should your present riches take to themselves wings, you would not be afraid to face uncertainty or poverty?

Madge. Not with you, Jack. Besides, poverty is such a little thing after all; and, so long as it does not enter our hearts, I wouldn't mind it a bit in my pocket.

Jack. Well, I don't know how it feels, for I have never been poor.

Madge (*surprised*). What do you mean?

Jack. That since I have always had your love, I am awfully sorry for the rich fellows. There is but one Madge in the whole world, you know.

Madge. And she is going to marry a Bohemian.

CURTAIN.

Druck:
Customized Business Services GmbH
im Auftrag der KNV-Gruppe
Ferdinand-Jühlke-Str. 7
99095 Erfurt